pisco sours

Ananda Esteva

CIVIL DEFENSE POETRY

Proofreading: Danielle Montgomery, Pablo Espinoza
Layout: Stephanie Heald
Cover Art: Fernando Martí

Library of Congress Control Number: 2006905614
Esteva, Ananda. 1971-
    Pisco Sours
    Poetry
    ISBN 978-0-9786913-1-8

Tree-free paper.

Reprint permission available upon request:
civildefensepoetry@gmail.com

Previously Published Works

"Poem For Robyn" was previously published in the Poetry
for the People anthology *Face America* (Poetry for the People
Press, Berkeley, Ca 1996). "When Latinos Go Buddhist"
was published in *Konch* online magazine (Ishmael Reed). A
different version of "Notification Of Baggage Inspection" was
recorded at KPFA Radio with co-author Solidad diCosta.
"Don't Know What To Say" was published in *Smartmouth*
(Writerscorps Books, San Francisco, Ca 2000). "This Is What
I'd Tell Her If We Were Friends Not Just Lovers" appears in
the Chicano zine, *La Llorona* (UC Berkeley, Berkeley, Ca
1996) and in *Conmoción #3 Identidad* (Tatiana de la Tierra, El
Paso, Tx 1996). "Eating Corn With Claudia" was published
in the chapbook *Manteca* (Galería De La Raza, San Francisco,
Ca). "Doesn't Matter What You've Lived Through, I Make
You Verde In My Arms" also appeared in *Molotov Mouths;
Explosive New Writing* (Jen Joseph, Manic D Press, San
Francisco, Ca 2003) as well as the anthology *Face America*
(Poetry For the People Press, Berkeley, Ca 1996). "Pisco
Sours" appears as prose within an essay entitled "¡Venceremos!
Words in Red Paint" in the anthology *Homelands: Women's
Journeys Across Race, Place, and Time* (edited by Patricia
Tumang & Jenesha de Rivera, Seal Press, Emeryville, Ca 2007).

table of contents

butterfly skin

i see the green blue jailhouse tattoo
on your forearm
a butterfly bathing in a deep inky pool
bleeding into yellow skin

i remember you told me that
your butterfly she sits
on a scar from their bullet
a snag
in the smooth golden plane of your arm
raised and twisted
lifting her left wing
blurring her blue design a bit

you notice my stare and point to her
you chuckle and grin
la mariposa— la transformación

remember this you said
didn't matter how much they tortured me
couldn't kill my spirit
fly high above them

the butterfly changes the pain that touches you beyond
your breath
that kidnaps you and
searches you with hot electric wires
turns your insides out
the butterfly she changes all that hurt into the power
to heal
into the power to laugh
to laugh
they can't take away my laughter
¡no pueden quitarme la risa!

in this tierra de conquista
(in this stolen land)

suavemente
bésame
que quiero sentir tus labios
besándome
otra vez
suavemente
bésame...

> — from "Suavemente" by Elvis Crespo

oye m'ijo
cántame suavemente
my body won't hear no other song
she's tired n' dried out
turning to prunes
the only fruit of this *tierra de conquista*
i need those gypsy tunes
native heartbeat
african rhythm
to heal my wounds
sew my skins together
with this sweet *merengue* song

sing me *suavemente*
a quiver from your vocal chords
falling on my skin
like feather fans of four cultures
fanning in *copal— salvia— cedro—* sweet grass
from four directions
to wake my mixed-blood soul
slowly drying up inside me
buried in the ashes of my ancestors
smothered by ashes of slash-n-burnt homelands
n' my soul locked up
with the shackles of every *africano*
stolen into slavery

just like this sweet *merengue*
a dance for slaves
combining *indio* flutes
west africa's *wolosodon*
and some spanish gypsy spice

merengue steps
silent
we can't wake the master
n' we can't break the chains
binding our feet

but we gotta dance
cuz nothing else gives us life
nothing else stops us
from drying up
our families
our bloodlines betrayed into slavery
then denied jobs
forced to live in toxic cities
where we sick
losing force
losing liquid
our blood drying up
turning into salt prunes— *saladitos*
in this *tierra de conquista*
where we all created equal on some paper nobody use

so dance me *suavemente m'ijo*
put your hand up on my hip n' look at me
hot lava in your eyes burn into mine
merengue all about *la miradita y la movida*
our legs sway together
just so
n' i swear there's a chain there
making us move as one
we turn constraints into *conjunto*

into *ritmo y pasito*
merengue all about making magic with the little we got
finding a freedom when we got none
fixing fluids to run thru my veins
cuz my blood dried up
for five hundred years now
when the first throat cut
in this *tierra de conquista*

so *báilame*
báilame suavemente m'ijo
don't let no chains stop you
from moving the way creator intended to
have you move with me
legs interlocked
your spirit touching up on every little *nido*
and forgotten spot
inside me
n' all we got is this moment
to parade thru the sky
like screaming eagles
tearing up *la tela del cielo*
with our cries
tearing up *la tela del cielo*
with our cries

we thunder through the heavens
and rain on the earth
giving more flow to the rivers
and when the music dies down
the air falls into silence
we sink down to the ground in our shackles
wet pieces of cloud
shroud our shoulders
but we're not beat down
no we're not beat down
we're just waiting
for the next
dance

modern healthcare in america

sick chicano baby of
single mother
worth less
than the cost to save his life

de-glorifying the mayflower

plymouth rock
place where pilgrims
first inserted
hard steel anchor
into the tender brown flesh
of turtle island

the general concern for immigrants crossing
an invented border between the usa &
méxico...

fifty spic bodies
shot down drowned in the river
río grande swells

república de chile, libertad

I loved collecting the Chilean coins of *diez pesos*, golden, embossed with a winged curvy woman standing triumphant, back arched, head up, arms outstretched above to some higher power, and chains dangling lifelessly from the cracked shackles on her wrists. She just broke free. Below her in bold capitals: *LIBERTAD*, LIBERTY. I wanted to **be** her. I wanted to embody her bold stance, feel the bristle of her muscles as she breaks through those irons. I collected a handful of those coins to covet in my ceramic Wells Fargo piggy bank. On days I felt trapped in our tiny apartment among large yelling voices and fears of going outside, I would take out a coin and look at her. *LIBERTAD*. She could fly me away.

Though I knew the basics for why we had left Chile, the details never came my way. I didn't know much besides some crazy family stories, leaving out all the parts my parents did not want to think about. If I had known more history, I would have thrown those coins away. For at the angel's hips were the numerals: 11-IX 1973; September 11th, 1973, the day Pinochet seized power, the day they stripped freedom from so many.

marching is a walking prayer

i gotta walk— walk
it's in my blood
my many ancestors walked
seems like i'm always going somewhere
i'm on the run
i can't even remember what from
my head gets so dizzy
i dash from thing to thing
so my head gets too dizzy
to think
to connect my soul to my body
to remember where i came from
my soul drifted off somewhere nodding out
drugged from the media-hype
trying to force me to forget
forget the bodies
the children my tax dollars kill
right now in the middle east
children walking walking walking
searching for water
searching for living family
contemplating US food drops over mine fields

which is the bigger risk
starvation or explosion?
and don't forget
missiles ravaging civilian homes
with **Made In The USA**
stamped into steel
as they try to stamp into our heads
the need for this unnecessary war
one minute
then a commercial for a fast car or SUV
and i start to forget about this war i just cried over
sometimes i even forget **his** face
the face of this man talking about infinite justice
his justice means our injustice
he's sitting there
talking about terrorism
terrorism from terrorist networks and
terrorism from the US military
but the military kind he calls civilization
he calls peace keeping
restoring order
how can i believe him when
this man has no lips
has no eyes
has no soul?

he talks hollow words
he lost his soul when his daddy killed bobby hutton
imprisoned peltier, mumia
dropped a bomb in philadelphia
he lost his soul when his family bought slaves
he lost his soul when they stole indian land
he lost his soul in the witch trials
he lost his soul during the crusades
he lost his soul
i have something to tell him
he lost his soul
and mine's off somewhere drifting away
drugged by the media-hype
i might forget what i want to say to this man
why would he listen to me anyway?
his ancestors didn't listen to my ancestors
mine run through me
cut deep into me
my ancestors
from all sides of the earth
urge me to walk— walk— walk
when i start to forget
when my head gets too dizzy to think
n' my soul is off somewhere nodding out
drugged from the media-hype

n' the bodies my tax dollars kill
fade from view
fade from view
fade from view like they never existed
fade from view
and my ancestors scream out
walk— walk!
but why?
i don't get it
what difference does a step make
does a turn of a wheel of a wheel chair
or the forward swing of a crutch?
why walk?

and then i remember
dolores huerta
five year ago at a rally in frisco
she said *marching is a walking prayer*
marching is a walking prayer
each step gives power to our prayer
and our words
our chants
our rhymes
our screams
give power to this prayer

let's pray together
let's walk together
each step
each turn
each forward swing of a crutch
each step
matters
marching is a walking prayer
a walking prayer that runs though
the generations

poem for robyn

doctor don't diagnose
when her leg bone run dry
he too afraid to touch her
big black woman
loving women
sent home
on crutches
painkillers
and prayer

un hermano moreno

told me
i got freedom cuz
i'm a seasonal
person of color
come winter
i fade off-white
güerita
passin' as a *gringa*
i got long latino hair but no gel
for my uniform
no gold
uniform
no hell–
red lips
no old–
school raiders jacket
drapin' at my hips
i don't stand target to white hate-crimes
like you *hermano*
true
hermano
but i got bullets in my gut too

hermano
bullets
rustin' in my gut
makin' me think i got nothin' worth tellin'
bullets rustin' n' tirin' me out
makin' me believe
what they tell me i can be
y nada más!

maybe
if this be **méxico**
we wouldn't blow around
homeless
burning tumbleweeds
without seeds for the future
maybe in **méxico**
we'd have less names dividing
chicano latino wetback *coyote* beaner spic hispanic
joto immigrant
fresh off the you-know-what sellout— *vendida*
names
hangin' round our dry burnt branches
maybe in **méxico**
our claw set deep in *nopales*
our *pueblo*

seguro
multicolorado
in ***méxico***
maybe me n' my skin wouldn't be
traitor to your cause
n' the red in your blood
not fade to pink
cuz of me
sittin' here writing this poem
standin' here reading this poem
tryin' ta knit my own roots with words
'fore i run out fists flyin'
i'm writin' tryin' ta find some
place
in this vast fast-land
some place to stand on my feet
n' hold hands
place where my checks won't bounce
where my house won't fall in
so i can feed folks with my food

maybe in ***méxico***
the earth will complete us
seep into our skins

settle the feuds between us
and within us
tide tensions between ancestors
indios irish african spanish
you know that way way back
the conquistadores
found power by robbing and raping
by pitting brother against brother against sister
and here we're tussling
doing their bidding some 500 years later

my name is ananda esteva
unadjusted mixed-blood immigrant to this land
and like you brother
i can't find where i came from
can't ignore where i came from
but you so busy staring at me
can't see the *aztlán* sun
behind you
its rays trying to touch you
its song trying to trickle into your ears
hoping to pass on a gift
el don del sol de aztlán
hermano— can you see it?

will you turn your head
outstretch your hands to accept this gift
or instead
will you point your finger at me?

tu alma mexicana, tu alma de café

now you say your folks named you "imogin"
for your irish grandma
your chicano cousins calls you *"imagen"*— for fun
cuz that's all you dare show these days... an image
of beauty in those cool new york fashion magazines!
you walk by and all we see is a petit plastic shell
you tan-skinned
itty-bitty-boned chick
chic and starving
hair gelled to vogue perfection
your name never sounding mexican
but exotic

in your hands you hold only
other people's opinions
gossip flows through your body
like one big gin binge
gushing in your mouth

oye imagen
when will you let warm *frijoles* pan-fried in *manteca*
flow through your frail frame?

please answer me
do i have to wait 'til your diet throws you into a gurney
dresses you in white
revealing the slight
brown in your skin?

during *fiestas* and family dinners
you make an excuse to leave the scene
or pick at the same *pepino* soaked in *chile* n' lime juice
all evening
smoking one *delicado* cigarette after another
family crowded all around you
meanwhile your eyes fixed somewhere so far away
i need a telescope to reach you
what do you see?
images of who you could never be
as pale as you're getting
you'll never make it to white
your features too broad— bountiful
even your hazel colored contacts can't hide
your big black eyes
a honey-colored partial eclipse of an onyx sun

sometimes as you float by
i check to see if your feet touch the ground

sometimes i see images of our past
your toothy grin framed by "wet 'n' wild"'s
darkest shades
my lipstick always crooked on the left
and those black *chola* bracelets we used to wear
that girl used to laugh and tell
the craziest *barrio* ghost stories ever!

oye imogin
imagen
i wish my embrace could bring back
tu alma mexicana
tu alma de café

when latinos go buddhist

my father decided to denounce the chastising laws of
catholicism
and embrace buddhism

in order to keep me on the path of awareness
he would say:

what's your problem ananda?
you're so spaced out
*you need to be **here***
present

take control of your mind
or others will

eh eh eh
it's here!

he even came up with his own terminology
we should call you... "dorpy"
cuz you're somewhere else
dorping around...

don't be tonta!

listen to me!
point your ears to this reality

aaaaaaay!
i caught you
drifting off ananda

wake up!

Duh-orpy!

i was a child
so used to following orders
i could not say
or even make the words
that i spaced out
to escape
him

notification of baggage inspection

To protect you and your fellow passengers, the
Transportation Security Administration (TSA) is required
by law...
(Section 110(b) of the Aviation And Transportation
Security Act of 2001.)
...to inspect all checked baggage.
As a part of this process, some bags are opened and
physically inspected. Your bag was among those selected
for physical inspection.

dear security inspector
i've been randomly searched...
again!

i know because my bag sports a plastic blue tag
a flag with a silver-colored emblem of your nation
the tsa transportation security administration
when i open my bag i see you leave
a written explanation
proof i can touch
like semen you been inside
my underwear

my clothes...you've seen my...condoms playing cards
personal organizer phonebook
shampoo sex toys sanitary napkins
notes to self
chapbooks lavender oil tooth brush hair brush
snot rags
sunglasses
sandwich wrappers
alcohol wipes and every single speck of that
nameless stuff at the bottom

dear security screener

thank you so much for inspecting my
bags again with dark baby blue
ties that divide our minds into
bicameral nightmares nowhere
and yet here
i wonder: this plastic tie sealing
the zipper on my bag... is it recycled?

i've been wondering how random is random when my
bags been searched 1,2,3,4,5 times in a row now
hmmm you think i didn't notice i was the only one

with the
hand written x on my security tag?

x marking the spot i represent to you
a dark unknown dangerous spot
haunting your day dreams during anti-terrorist trainings
your x brands me
replaces my middle name

Ms. Ananda X. Esteva,
may I have your passport?

i remember how you held my passport and ticket
in one hand
out of my reach
asking me intimate questions about my uncle in
south america
where exactly does he live now...
how many countries did he live in...
but behind your sweet cheek dimple
i know you know he fled chile— bolivia— *perú*
after killing a sergeant in self-defense
i gotta keep talking
so i don't sound suspicious

but i'm afraid to say too much
the glint from your white teeth blind me as pickpocket
hands reach
deep into my cavities
searching for secrets

i try to walk invisible
past your watch
through your gates
i wanna leave no trace
on the rice paper path behind me
walk quiet

no matter what that spiritual song says
i gotta douse the little light of mine shining
to blend in so i look like
all the other dead people around here
who forgot to stop and ask questions

but then the grass green light goes off at your security
station
you got me
going through secondary inspection
again

i've already been marked
see
i got this scar on my forehead
an x etched in
that follows my path through data streams
flowin' through data bases
flowin' as ink on tickets with special numbers
these numbers carry instructions
for you to recognize me as a threat to order and safety

now if you read time magazine
from back in the 70's
that's all general *pinochet* wanted to do

restore order

the order time said was caused by socialist chaos
too many free thoughts
working to feed the hungry
too many factories owned by workers
refusing to give a cut to the US

but i know that's the same order
that sent students running through the streets
fleeing from your bullets

order that makes mamas cry
all night clutching photos of their disappeared children
if i am a threat to this order
then so be it

TSA sincerely regrets having to search your bag.
Before your next trip visit our web site!
We appreciate your understanding and cooperation.

"Notification of Baggage Inspection" was co-written
with poet Solidad diCosta

chulo-feo

you could say
i walked away
from you
played giraffe
stretched my neck high
above you and
split— bye
but *mi chulo-feo*
can you sense how your boiling breath
lingers in my throat
smells of deep
green leaves from the jungle?
your breath
clouds my eyes like you
the churning geyser and
me the brisk night sky
mixing with you
making a thick amber steam
that gathers in the hairs between
my legs and sticks there
if you know what i mean

you may say i walked away
but i'm hanging off the tip of your tongue
right now
sipping on your memory
when you black out it's me
indulging in our thick-fingered embraces
i remember how they singed my clothes
and burned me to the bone
my marrow melted into puddles
while you held
me
n' i won't let go
of your touch
chulo
i can't let go when a winter storm be
blowing thru my body
rattling rib against rib
twisting kidneys n' liver together
making a massacre of my innards
winter
been raging through my body too long and only you
can thaw my bitter history

don't you know you
and your growling geyser fit inside me

like the sun does in the sky
and when i walk away
with my proud step
it's only to say
chulo
don't
leave me behind

street signs

All those years married to my *tía*, the first time
Uncle went to Chile was to bury her ashes, back in the
country of her birth. That was her wish. Really, her
wish was to see her country at least once before dying
but the cancer swept through her so fast that only in
ash-form could she return. Uncle knew little Spanish,
enough to crack a few jokes: *Tres Tristes Tigres Tragaron
Trigo en un Trigal.*

But the task of getting permission to bury her
in the family mausoleum was larger than quoting
Condorito or reciting childhood tongue twisters. After
17 years of a right-wing dictatorship, the only thing
allowed to remain red in Chile was the tape. Stamp-
wielding officials loved to say No! Maybe Nancy
Reagan had campaigned there, too.

So Uncle offered to pay for my plane fare and
hotel, if I could help him, guide him, his 21st century
Sacagawea to forge through the world of Chilean
funerary bureaucracy.

When I met him at the airport, he had already
memorized his Chilean travel guide. He knew so
much, rattling off bits of history and things to see, it

was as if he and *Tía* had visited her homeland every few years or so. More important than that, he knew enough to hold his tongue not just to say what came to mind.

The next day, he asked me if I noticed: so many street signs named *"Avenida Once De Septiembre"* Avenue Of September 11th. His book showed similar signs in cities scattered from south to north... small cities and even a collection of touristy towns. Rumors of Brazilian Carnival floats featuring paper mache puppets of Bin Laden and Bush duking it out, poking fun at the 9/11 tragedy, had already reached us by then. "Is Chile in favor of 9/11?" He asked in a hushed voice. Looking around to make sure no one heard.

"No." I said.

"That was the day of the coup d'état when they bombed the Chilean equivalent of the White House and General Pinochet seized power. They named those streets after September 11th 1973. Weird, huh?"

Through his clear gray eyes, I watched his mind spin this information around, break it apart and put it back in order. I wonder if it struck him as strange that this country publicly celebrated the offing of its own president. Imagine streets entitled John Wilkes Booth or Lee Harvey Oswald Parkway... *Once De*

Septiembre: these signs said Chile honored the power
of the dictatorship and the handshake with the United
States that funded it. I can hear the endorsements
now: "This *coup d'état* was made possible by a generous
contribution from the C.I.A."

Forty million American dollars later, the people
who didn't agree with these events, those people could
not publicly express their opinions... bound by hush
and whispers and silence... Those people became
afraid to sing folk songs, and afraid to play traditional
music, and their history systematically unwritten...
Those were, perhaps, the same people who turned and
rushed away when I tripped and tasted the dust of the
cobblestone roads in downtown Santiago, afraid that by
helping me back up, they would endanger themselves.
I don't blame them. Every day, they were reminded
that Chile is not their country anymore, not the way
it used to be. The words to the folk song that goes
"Chile lindo y querido..." drowned out by the droning
of progress: a partnership with the USA. Those signs
reminded all passers-by that Chile was for those who
agreed with September 11, 1973... for the people who
willingly frequented the new Mc Donald's or some
other Mc *Yanqui* franchise, as American corporations
rolled in like a biting, sinister breeze. The new Chile

was for the people who thought folk music was hokey and Indian people were ugly so who cares if the new government bombed their villages? "If that even happened... And the disappeared, the dissidents did not die." As one of my father's friends had pointed out: "They were offered land in Brazil and resettled there, in the warmth of the Amazon Basin."

In downtown plazas placed throughout the country, signs saying, *"Once De Septiembre"* reigned. I imagine that witnessing those signs, silently divided the country. Opinions seasoning, but never tasted. For one half, the signs reminded them of the glorious day Chile walked out of the caves and accepted modernity. For the other, those signs acted like arthritis, a cold ache in the bones, as that bitter, sinister breeze rolls in from the north. Memories of a lost loved one, someone presumed dead, their body never returned home, flash like lightning. The northern storm stretches out across the sky, raining hail and sleet... stinging skin. September 11th was a chokehold: submit or be submitted... shut up and take it.

I wonder had *Tía* lived long enough to see her country, if she would have liked what she saw: a country trying so hard to be like the United States, a country riddled with hatred and holes created by that

biting, burrowing wind? Oh and this wind so familiar
now, it shoots through the city near-silent. It slips
into the background like white noise. Everyday people
throughout the country pass by those signs inscribed:
Once De Septiembre, celebrating the assassination of
president Allende, elected so long ago, it seems like a
dream. As pedestrians pass by those street signs, that
northern wind enters their bodies silently separating
Chile's people, ripping holes into hearts and other vital
organs. The pain choked out by the analgesic glitter of
consumerism, as another American mall stands up tall,
through the wreckage of fallen buildings full of holes.

don't know what to say

what do i tell her
my student
comes to class
bloodied and bruised
by her boyfriend
by her girlfriend
do we talk about it
as a class topic
or do i attract and distract
with some other fact of
life
like political prisoners
or how to sample your favorite song in your poem
or anything
anything
but let's not talk about how bad you look
bloodied and bruised
and how i wish i could have been there
take the weapon out of his and her hands
i won't show you
i'm screaming inside and

how much i wanna cry
and you don't either

what do i tell her
my student
comes to class
bloodied and bruised
by her boyfriend
by her girlfriend
how do i convince her
the pencil
writing words
can free her
not from life's whipping winds
and the burn they make on her skin
but free her mind
from stopping to think
she deserve it?

this is what i'd tell her if we were friends not just lovers

i only like girls who look like girls she says
and i'm watching her like for the first time
i examine her rind
her broad-shouldered letterman jacket
her gelled up crew cut
i listen
to the teenage boy sound in her voice like she swallows
her words b-fore they come out
but don't you like yourself? i ask
secretly wishing to dig out her insides
i wanna know!
well yeah she says
and that's all i can get out of her
sometimes i call her *mi hombrecito* my little man
just to make her smirk
i'll do anything to rise a reaction!
i'm her sourdough starter and
she's so quiet
stoic
like a man

and i wanna know does she love herself and
i wanna tell her she's beautiful
but i bet no one ever called her that before and
if they did
would she believe them?
i'm starting to wonder what the hell people think
beauty is anyway
but it's not tomboy
not jock
not a buzz cut with a low croaking voice to match
i don't know her world
once as the sun was rising and she looked at me sweaty
weary
i got a flash of her future
a time when she believes in herself
believes in her ability to draw
in that flash i saw light pour in around her
n' caress the walls of her studio
sprawling with drawings and murals
and she smiles at me lightly
she feels complete
then i sunk back to the moment
i was naked and she in her tank top in my bed
i could see and feel her womanhood that morning
after we killed each other with our fingers and tongues

and teeth

ay como me matas! round after round

i can't get enough

it's those times when she tells me 'bout her family

in san diego and her love she left there

those times when her thick skin falls to her side and

she dares express herself

i live for those moments

she only likes girls

who look like girls but

does she like herself

and as we walk down the street

i look at her

and she's a mystery

a genderfuck

forever silent

mi hombrecito— my little man

i wanna tell her she's beautiful

but i don't dare

the third seat

Uncle carried *Tía's* ashes in a brown cardboard box about the size to fit a fat bottle of Port or about half the length of a rationing of government cheese. Her box was heavier than the port and cheese put together. But it's just **ashes** right? Aren't ashes supposed to be light, flying like little wings after a fire? Her box pulled me down, anchored my body and dizzied my head. Maybe it's got her memories trapped inside. My mind wandered while I held it. *Tía* weighed over 200 pounds in life... so in a way, this box is nothing. And maybe nothing is inside it, nothing that matters, just dried out scraps of flesh and bone. I want to think her spirit **did** lift up on little wings or merge with the green of the earth, tropical and warm like a hearty sigh. I want to believe this box held **only** the rind that held her.

Uncle wanted to be efficient. We envisioned taking care of the paperwork and burying her all on the same day. Only the engravings would take time, and with a little bribery, that time would shrink down too. So as we began our journey, we woke up early and we brought *Tía's* box to breakfast. When the waitress came to greet us, Uncle requested a table for three. She looked at him and she looked at me and shrugged. "These Americans need a lot of space." I am guessing she was thinking. We sat down, one chair for me, one for him and one for *Tía's* box. She sat on the far side of the table, **almost** out of view. We ordered. The choices limited. This particular restaurant focused more on spirits of the alcoholic kind and evening soccer games on T.V. The waitress brought us our food. My Uncle, who loves to tell jokes, thanked her for the food and then gestured to the box. "My wife won't be eating anything." He said and I translated. Her whole body hiccupped. Wondering if she didn't get it, he slapped the box playfully with his hand and said in Spanish, *"Mi esposa."* My wife. The waitress sucked in the sides of her cheeks and then slowly backed up, one high-heeled foot, then another, as if following wilderness survival instructions: "When stumbling upon a rattlesnake, slowly back up. Do not turn around and run away." When it came time for our check, another waitress served us. The first one disappeared. Maybe she got bit after all.

I haven't tried this experiment in the United States; bring a box of someone's ashes and tour the country, diner after diner just to document people's reactions. But in Chile, our journey to the cemetery we thought would take one day, dragged out for nine, and even **then** we didn't finish! As we toted *Tía's* remains around town giving her seats at every table, most people reacted the same way: wide eyes, twisted faces frozen in time, and an occasional quivering finger pointing our way.

Maybe they thought her box **did** hold memories or feelings of resentment for a life cut short and these things could seep out and harm them. Or perhaps they believed the simple unrest of body out of the earth would haunt them at night, sucking away their sleep.

Why Uncle made an effort to announce to everyone we came across, "Meet my wife." I haven't worked it out yet. I'm guessing he missed her. Sometimes, I could tell by the disdain in people's eyes, they saw us as disrespectful, soiling the memory of a good woman. "These are not things to do in public." Hell, we weren't career criminal urn-robbers. We were just trying to bury *Tía*, stumbling over mounds of paper as we trekked from government office to office. Oh yes, by the end, we saw the whole of old Santiago.

I like to think that *Tía* enjoyed the ride, revisiting the city, taking in the sumptuous smells of Chilean *casuela seca, empanadas*, and *pastel de choclo*, oh, and an occasional *Pisco* Sour. I heard spirits like strong scents and food and drink. I think spirits like being talked about, remembered, and we sure remembered her as we went. I wonder if she laughed when Uncle forgot to bring her certificate of death papers, marriage license, and other essential documents we tried to get faxed over from the US. Yes, she took care of all those things for him. Did she feel touched when at the beach Uncle and I started crying until he chanted out: **Dos** *Tristes Tigres Tragaron Trigo En Un Trigal,* with us being the **two** sad tigers, turning our sobs into chuckles? I wonder, did she laugh too? Yet some doubt swirls within me like a dusty cloud. As I straddle two identities, Chilean and American, I can't figure out if we disrespected her or blessed her with visceral offerings and tacky jokes. The mystery rides on through the night. I wonder if Uncle ever lost sleep over this. For now, I sleep okay.

i got delays in my paycheck and hunger in my bones

delays in my paycheck
delays in my paycheck make me eat too much
at my friend's house
my fork shows no discrimination
half-cooked *menudo* coleslaw and spam pickled
ham hocks
all taste good
i can't stop
get giddy when i feel the taught knot in my stomach
'bout to burst
i know
i should lay down
let my tum disperse
oh it hurts
but i need that full feeling
delays in my paycheck make me
need that full feeling
and i don't stop with food
delays in my paycheck
make my close friends
smell so good!

right now *m'ijo*
you're my closest friend
so i hope you comprehend my hunger
for you
your scent screams through my nose
like white waters rushing over rocks
kisses i lay on your face
taste like hot *enchiladas*
baked in thick green sauce
delays in my paycheck
make me lap up your sauce
imbibe your smile
stretch my pores to receive the shine in your eyes
packed with ultraviolet rays to
radiate my cancerous residues
caused by waking up worried 'bout rent n' food
i said waking up worried 'bout rent and food
where the hell am i gonna find the money?!
how far will i fall this time?
so i need food to undo my worries
i need you
to drown the delays in my paycheck
with your sweet *salsa*
i got delays in my paycheck and hunger in my bones
homes
so you better like me plump!

54

our little freedom poem

To Alegría Barclay.

ay ay ay alegría
as we walk down the street
hummingbirds fly in our hair
hover at our lips
cuz if they could talk in words
we'd sound like them
our voices mingle like waterfall and the river
some kinda current
running figure eights between us
everybody see
all we can do not to rocket to the sky
and leave this earth behind
we fluid like quicksilver
and we carry its movement within
our bodies
we got a freedom
nobody take away
if only just for today
we got something honey
heads turn as we walk

two femmes hand in hand
flowing in n' out of each other's step
a dance we knew as children
flowing from holding
and being held
telling daytime dreaming stories
traveling together
back home— home— home
switching between lands
as we walk hand in hand
you vietnam
and me chile
switching our hips as we walk
and heads turn
when we switch our hips
as we walk
stepping like deer
like fawns in the early summer
full of play
and *verde que te quiero verde pa' siempre*
that's right
we won't dry up dead like pulled up weeds
i said we won't
dry up dead like pulled up weeds
though we be pulled up weeds

our roots transplanted again and again
our many bloods
many grandmothers
swirling inside us
and it's survival
to keep switching
between lands
you vietnam
and me chile
switching our hips as we walk
switching our stance sometimes
'til we know it's safe to speak our minds

together we find a freedom
rare as the rain forest
and as deep
and as delicate
together we got something
nobody take away
we go switch switch switchin'
and if you mess with us
we'll take a switch to you
cuz we hard as we are soft
and yes we do
switch in bed

our lovers confused as they watch us walk away together
two femmes hand in hand
flowing in n' out of each other's step
a dance we knew as children
flowing from holding and being held
telling daytime dreaming stories
and listening
traveling together
back home— home— home
wherever that home is
we don't really know
alegría
this our little freedom poem
the only place
we'll find our freedom
on paper

eating corn with claudia

Sometimes magical realism is our reality.

eating corn with claudia
walking to the oaktown corner store
we trying to snatch us some smokes
tryin' to get us somewhere
yeah when our chit chat get growing
like pole-beans at dusk
grown so big
they block out the city
up to the moon!
and lamp posts sprout leaves
and roads relax
to red earth
and curbs turn to fields
wavin' in the breeze
yeah we may gnaw our corn to the bone
but see it still glow yellow
n' plump between the tips of our fingers
n' for a moment the scent of chile n' honduras
lingers
in our noses

oaktown turns to **our town**
while i'm eating corn with claudia
oaktown turns to **our town**
n' for once— we feel full

doesn't matter what you've lived through
i make you "verde" in my arms

verde
*que te quiero **verde***
green i want you green
when i say *verde*
i'm not just talking about the color
and *lorca*
the guy who cried these words the first time
he had other things on his mind

verde** que te quiero **verde
***verde** carne*
***verde** pelo*

i want your body
green as the last jungle canopy
i want your skin green
your hair
i want your touch
green like a meadow in the springtime
now do you know what i mean?
green isn't just a color

it's a way of saying
i'm fresh and plump on the vine
and i'm firm
mr. noonday sun hasn't beaten me down to a pulp
cuz i won't let him

some people say **verde** for unripe fruit
but baby it's our word now
and i'm telling you i'm **verde** not
cuz i been hiding behind a leaf
my whole life
when i was 16 i thought i'd seen it all
i let boys do whatever they wanted
with my body
i let girls say whatever they wanted
about my body
i wasn't **verde**
n' i carried them with me
i carried them with me
in my tired swollen body
*pero te digo que estoy **verde***
***verde** viviente*

green like hot summer rain
tearing through your clothes
running down your body
hot summer rain is *verde*
and you know i'm feeling *verde*

just ease into the *verde* breeze
doesn't matter what you've lived through
i make you *verde* in my arms
verde carne
verde piel

pisco sours

When I went back to Chile in 1987, there existed no place to express your opinions, emotions, songs... but I remember seeing one wall spray painted in fierce red, ¡Venceremos! We will win! The wall chipped and pockmarked from rounds of bullets like tooth-marks from a hungry creature aiming to keep people silent.

i'm on my way to *el mercado central*
indoor shopping for folks with not a whole lot of
money to spend
i walk across the four wide lanes of *la alameda*

five canvas covered vehicles roll by
i step onto the sidewalk
one truck jumps up the curb
blocking my way
i see young men in the back manning what looks to me
like a bazooka
never stand behind a horse
never stand in front of a bazooka!

but i don't have much choice as the space between the
truck and the wall narrows
i can't go back because
more canvas trucks roll up behind me
as i inch around the heavily armed butt of this vehicle
a young man tilts the cannon's projectile away from
the sky
and points it toward me

seeing the horror on my face
he looks me in the eye and grins
he looks deranged like after too many sleepless nights
at that moment i am his and he knows it and he enjoys
this knowledge tremendously
he's caught me in his web of killing-gadgets
i am one more conquered bitch
one more notch
one more clumsy drunken story after a night of
pisco sours
pisco sour is the national drink of chile and
i'm sure **he** felt he represented the nation
he got to be a **special** protector
one who would really put his back into his work
if you know what i mean

yes he'll go all the way
to prove his loyalty

he— a darker-skinned man in a country trying to be
european
where class-lines and color-lines intersect
he— young with some education
but not too much to slow down his actions
to allow him to question the orders
given to him by lighter-skinned men
with more status and more protections
those men stake claim to a purely european pedigree
he cannot touch

i can tell by the look in his eyes
he is ready to breathe life into his orders and
execute them on a personal plane
yes very personal
i don't break my gaze with him
i don't dare
his eyes tell me
if there were an alley near by...
i would be there
pinned under him...

his buddies 'round the corner to back him up
pretending not to look
oh what stories they'll tell tonight over shots of *pisco*
what patriots
putting a subversive tramp in her place!
you don't look the military in the eyes
and get away with it
and i wished i didn't look like those women at *café haiti*
serving coffee in skin-tight stretch dresses
with my curves so freely flowing as i walk
i learned to strut like the girls in my neighborhood back
home
holding waists making a soul-train
singing *in my house— in my house...*
but i know i'm not in my house anymore
this is **his** house and his rule and he
can decide to set off that cannon right into my middle
just because he feels like it
just because he's got something to prove

i am on his turf and he knows it
that much he can claim
and this chile this faraway place i called home
for 15 years

what does it matter?
standing between his cannon and a wall
i have nothing
this chile
this home i hopcd would **shelter** me...
let in all the cold night air and wicked winds to rattle me
around
rip out my roots

but as i stand there between the vast black hole of his
cannon
and the stone wall behind me
as i stand there
i recall the wall with the word *¡venceremos!*
spray-painted in red
growing up in the US
i don't even know what it means
but that word gives me hope *¡venceremos!* we will win!
that's the same word
spray-painted all over town
when *allende* won the presidency in 1970
lasting three years before the right snatched it away with
bombs and kilos of greenbacks

i know somewhere inside of me i have to **be** that word
¡venceremos!
despite all those years playing coy and invisible
giving others what they wanted
no— i gotta find a way to breathe life into it
just as he has to breathe life into his orders to inflict
terror
i have to be red
strong
with an exclamation point at my side
like the spear my *indio* grandfather not allowed to keep
i can walk with it now
i can strut and sway the way my body's made to
if i feel like it
i have to win
the right to return to my homeland without being
under fire

then i remember the pockmarks surrounding that word
marks from rounds of bullets forced into that wall again
and again
they could have painted over that word
but they figured leaving it among bullet holes made

a stronger message:
you can try but you can never win!
i'm thinking somebody died for that word just as victor
jara died for his song

but after fifteen years of patrolling people's voices
military forgot about the power of the word
the words of the people
despite the bullet holes
you can still read that word clearly
in red you can see the hurried but bold letters emerge
from spray-painted lines: *¡venceremos!*
that's right
we will win!
and words i know are powerful
so many cultures believe the world started with words
poems

so what if i start with this poem— *¡venceremos!*
i don't have to understand it
what if i stare into the night of his cannon
and instead of death
i see red smoke snaking out
writing in the air like spray paint graffiti
writing me a new ending to this story?

and those words— this poem— grabs me by the waist
shields me
whisks me away from his cannon
his backup
and as i walk
with red words wrapped around me
my hips can swerve and sway up and down the block
and it don't matter
cuz nobody can touch me now!

Without These People, This Book Wouldn't Be

DJ Javier, James, Julie, Lauren, Dani, Jenny-Goose, Gramma V. Bea, Waldo, Dre-Dog, Andy, Diane-Julya, Norma-June, Maiana, Kirsten Thomas, Cindy, David, Lynn, Tina, Caryn, Wayne, Connie, Shawna, Saúl, Leroy, Josiah, Chavín de Huántar, and June & the old ones.

Ananda Esteva was born in Chile and raised in the San Francisco Bay Area. She works as an elementary school teacher. She has taught poetry with the East Bay Institute for Urban Arts, Digital Underground Story Telling, June Jordan's Poetry for the People, and Writers' Corps. She has toured across North America several times. Her writing weaves in a duality of culture, perspective, sexuality, and language. Ananda is currently working on a memoir detailing her first trip back to Chile in 1987 during Pinochet's dictatorship.

photo: Juliette Monheit